Table For One

Encountering His Reveal

Joyce,
Think you for being
my amazing woman called
by God! I wish you the best
for your book!

Lahoma Dade

Lahoma Dade

Scriptures taken from the Holy Bible, New International Version®, NIV®.Copyright © 1973, 1978, 1984 by Biblica, Inc.™ Used by permission of Zondervan. All rights reserved worldwide.
www.zondervan.com
Scripture quotations marked NLT are taken from the Holy Bible, New Living Translation, copyright 1996, 2004. Used by permission of Tyndale House Publishers, Inc., Wheaton, Illinois 60189. All rights reserved.
Scripture quotations marked "NKJV" are taken from the New King James Version. Copyright © 1982 by Thomas Nelson, Inc. All rights reserved. Used by permission.
Scripture references that do not have Bible version noted are either acknowledged in the footnote or the author's paraphrase.

Cover design by Love and Change Studios
Book design by Love and Change Studios
www.loveandchange.com
All rights reserved.

Lahoma Dade
Visit my website at www.tableforonebook.com

Library of Congress Control Number: 2010915849

First Printing: October 2010
ISBN-13 9780615411507

Printed in the United States of America

Acknowledgments

$\mathcal{M}$y number one cheerleader, my Mom, Audrey. My amazing pastors, mentors and role models Cheryl Luke, Cissy Luke, Earl and Oneka McClellan, Pastors Rob and Laura Koke and the staff at Shoreline Church in Austin, TX.

My dad Homer Dade and my awesome step-mom, Reneta Dade. My grandma, Kathleen Williamson. My older brothers Corey and Steve Dade. Those with whom I am leaving my legacy: Malcolm, Mikayla and Kathy Dade. Andrea, Brianna, Claudia, Jaydon, Joy and April Williamson, Shakena Powell, Mya Steward.

The best editor in the world Brittany Laneaux of Love and Change Studios in Austin,TX. I cannot leave out my other set eyes Shontaye Bowman, Angie Gatewood and Andrea Moore. The woman who can dress me better than I can dress myself, Lucy Cabrerra. My amazing photographers Adrian Gutierrez and Maryna Marsten.

My amazing girlfriends who keep me sane, love every part of me and keep me near the Cross: Carla Jones, Shavon McNack, Lena Daniels, Evelina Solis, Melissa Gray, Jessica Mercado, DavRena Williams, Jennifer Eguagwu, Nere Emiko, Salli Dennis, Emily Gipson, Meagan Armstrong, Rian Carkhum, Ashley James, Judy Kassaye, Tamra Cobbins, Nadine Matthews, Felicia Matthews, Sharan Robinson, Analicia Trevino, Jennifer Contreras, Ashley and Krystal Stephney, Robin Dotson, Tammi Douglas, Kristina Adams, Barbara Salisbury, Leah Campos, Autumn Konopka, Zoe Ann Heep, Chika Anosike, Adesewa Faleti, Falana Thomas, Emmalyn Wang, Erika Gonzalez, Marcella DeLuna, Kristina Adams, Ruth Luke, Tiffany Stewart, Gretchel Dixon, Judy Brown, Diane Umana, Graciela Solis, Jessica Walls, Ruth Byington, Sarah Bownds, Kathleen Denyer, Heidi Kelly, Marilyn Butler, LeStar Cofer, Sommer and Kinesha Rogers Melissa Young, Jamie Burkett and Tatiana Williamson

My amazing brothers in Christ who have shown me so many things on so many levels including the way I deserve to be treated: Derrek Luke, Doug Young, Chad Steadham, Nick Traylor, Tyrone Thompson, Onome Ufomata, Elie Taylor, Jason Aleem, Ron Orisma, Martin Egwuagu, Johnie Jones III, Brandon Brison, Randy Williamson, Kai Williamson, Tauren Thompson, Vincent Harding, Corey Harrison, Chadwick Sapenter, Dan Behnke, Curtis Bradford, Curtis Retherford, Jonathan Dixon, Stephen Contreras, Will Matthews, James Jacobs, Shadrick Bell, Marcus Herford, Kevin Starr, David Lawrence, Tobin Hurley, Ramon Solis, Luke Koke, Fathom Kimes, Chris Hamlin, Ron Brown, David Reiner and James Jacobs.

Introduction

Welcome to the table. Please have a seat.

I left the plate empty in front of you as I lay out ten distinctively unique courses for you to indulge in at your own pace. Tackling each one daily or weekly is suggested. This book can be read either independently or in a group and has been set up so that you can get the most out of the experience. This interactive encounter is a testament to God's character and His desire for you to be fully whole, healed, and restored. God has reserved a place specifically for you that will keep you coming back for more.

This encounter is purposefully established through thoughts, scriptures, and personal reflection that provides revelations of who He is in hopes that it will catapult you into a renewed sense of forgiveness, wholeness, freedom and trust in Him.

His timing is impeccable. His words are true. Open your heart and mind to allow Him to minister to you in the unseen areas. God will cover you with His colors to reveal a beautiful mosaic that displays His grace, love and mercy throughout this interaction. What you are hungry for, He will fulfill.

Sit back as I take you on a journey and God will provide the encouragement you need to finish strong.

Contents

Encounter One:
The Slopes

My best friend plans our vacations, and this year she decided that we would get a group together and take it to the slopes, the beautiful mountains of Lake Tahoe, Nevada! On this particular vacation, we took a small army with us. Well, it felt that way, especially with all the bags and ski equipment. I knew very little about the people in the group and even less about skiing, but I trusted my best friend not to lead me in the wrong direction. The snow capped scenery was breath taking; there were mature, sturdy trees holding up blankets of thick crisp white snow. In wonderment, we curved around turn after turn to arrive at our destination, a perfectly positioned, snow enveloped winter home.

We settled in. Immediately we explored this huge winter home and started enjoying the company of one another. The conversations were intimidating: unknown elements, altitude, lift, runs, slopes, colors, falling off mountains and bears! It dawned on me that I was totally out of my element. All I could think was that I had no idea what I got myself into! As they fearlessly discussed plans for the following day's adventure, I quietly withdrew upstairs to gain the courage needed to take on this new experience.

The morning came quickly, and the moment of doom arrived when one of the ladies asked, "What are you going to do today?" "I am staying here at the house; I plan to take in all the scenery," I replied merrily! They all chuckled; "Yeah right, No really?" "I am going skiing with you!" I replied as the chuckle turned into an outburst of laughter. "I am not a teacher, I'm a skier!" They clearly thought I needed another option. My best friend, who is very perceptive, flipped through the ski school books to find an early lesson for me.

Since this was my first time in this environment, I was ill-prepared for the cold, much less skiing. The ladies let me borrow some of their extra gear as I reminded them that 'we' are tropical people. By the time I hit the door, I looked like I stepped right out of a giant crayon box, red, white, and grey jacket, black jumpers, brown boots, purple scarf, black gloves and orange glasses! I laughed at myself while hearing my mom's voice echo in the back of my head, "Make due with what you have!"

Arriving for the lessons 15 minutes early, a miracle in itself, they wouldn't let me in the first class! All the other participants followed the ski school instructions and arrived more than an hour early. Although I negotiated to no avail with a pimple-faced boy behind the counter, he did not budge on the rules. Without a class, I was left to fend for myself in this new uncharted territory, and those mountains were much bigger up close. Instead of trying my luck, I headed back to the house.

Upon arriving back at the house, I began the strenuous process of undressing as I removed all of my crayon-colored gear, also known as borrowed ski attire, piece by piece. Quickly the peace and quiet turned creepy as I sat in the huge house alone. The cold unfamiliar outdoor elements were more appealing than being isolated in that huge house. I searched through the ski books to find the next lesson time, got re-dressed and ventured back out in the elements again. This late class meant that I would have very little time left to ski, if any, but I was fine with that.

I returned to the same counter. This time I collected both my lift and ski school tickets. Next, I got fitted for my skis! Being on the skis made me think of all the possible calamities that could take place: running into a kid, falling off the side of a mountain, or just not being able to stop. I did not want to take any chances, so I slid my way down the common area and patiently waited for my ski school class to begin.

In class, I learned to slide, stop, turn, fall gracefully and some other important things. After learning the basics, my class and I went to a self contained training area called the Lessons Slope. It was low, smooth and wide with barriers all around for safety. I gained confidence in my ability to ski by repetitively going back up the lesson slope. By the end of the class, I was ready to take on any mountain or, so, I thought. As the day winded down, the slopes closed. Bright and early the following morning, they better be ready because "Watch out slopes, I am coming for you!!"

The next morning was electric as we all began the day together. Time to hang with the big girls! Map in hand, my best friend led the way back up the slopes. I trusted her ability to ski but failed to take into account her ability to read a map! We reached the top of this majestic mountain together which instinctively caused us to pause for a moment to take it all in. Filled with courage and excitement, we were on top of the world!

We began to descend down the mountain at a smooth, slow and steady pace, just like any smart amateur would! My best friend's mapping abilities, I came to realize, were non-existent! Unfortunately, we arrived at the top of the red advanced slope before we discovered that we were totally off course for the green beginner slope. There was only one way down, so I had no choice except to go! Off I went, crashing and burning every 10 seconds. The spectators, including my best friend, kept me from staying down. Every time I crashed, I got back up! The mile stretch that should have taken about four minutes took me about an hour. This partially was not my fault; after all, if she read the map properly, we would have been on the green, easy slope.

Insistently after what felt like my 50th fall, I asked my best friend to go ahead and ski without me; I did not want to ruin her fun. She finally obliged after having to almost hurt her feelings to do so. Momentarily, I would accelerate, and after a few seconds I would get afraid all over again, clip my skis together and fall. Over and over and over again! Tired of falling, I broke the number one ski school rule; I plummeted with my skis straight out, head first down a portion of the run. It only lasted for about 30 seconds before I literally rolled like a huge bowling ball from the top to the bottom level of the run. Luckily, my borrowed gear provided enough cushion to avoid any broken bones. I slowly gathered my pride and composure to get back up after this terrifying roll. A few skiers who witnessed the roughage kindly returned my skies and quickly darted on down the mountain.

I had enough with this whole skiing thing, or so I thought, I would overcome this run, even if I had to walk. That's exactly what I did; I walked down a good part of the next run. Swiftly, I realized that it was extremely difficult to walk on the ledge of a cliff with snow up to my thighs. After I walked for a short time, the top half of my body was scorching hot with the sun beating down while the lower half of my body was tired and freezing cold. All I want to do was hurry up and get down; I regained the courage to put the skis back on. In the distance, I could see that I had quite a ways to go before I could get to the ground level.

Cautiously and slowly, I rounded the corner where I did the ultimate no-no again and set my skis straight, not even considering that this is the way to get to top speed. I heard a loud snap when I suddenly realized that the snap was me. I found myself motionless on my back; I hit dead center into the middle of a huge tree! There was no way, if I could even move, that I was going to get back up and attempt to ski again.

Very nice people came to my rescue advising me not to move as they motioned for a medic to come. Afraid that every bone in my body could be broken, I laid still in the freezing cold, flat on my back. When the medic arrived, he wrapped me like a taco on a flat stretcher as he pulled me behind him down to the ground level of the slope to safety. Luckily, I walked away unharmed. Nothing broken. Needless to say, I have yet to plan another trip to the slopes.

Reflecting later, I realized that every part of this experience meant something; it was more than just a trip, falls, maps, friends and being wrapped like a taco! It symbolized so many things in the season that I was in. Falling every 10 seconds correlated to the number of times that I have blown it, messed up and completely failed. Although I have taken a lot of falls that the enemy would like me to focus on, the more symbolic part of the fall was the number of times that I got back up. I have made my own map time after time and seen the wrong side of many mountains, but no matter where I ended up, there was a way to get off. I had to go through some things and pay some consequences for my choices. In this experience I allowed my pride and desire to not show any sign of weaknesses, to let me go down the slopes all alone. There may not have been a need for a medic had I not felt like I could take on something like this huge slope and small runs in my own strength. In the end, the medic, Jesus was right there to pick me up and place me back on solid ground. He comes when I have had the falls, the breaks, and the slams because that is when I finally trust him enough to surrender. No matter the situation, he always comes to wrap me up, clean me off and put me back on solid ground.

Prayer

God I thank you that you are the same God at the top of the mountain as you are at the bottom. Thank you that no matter where I am, you are there. Your strength is made perfect in my weakness, and I confess that I am weak. Show yourself strong. Teach me to acknowledge you in all my ways and not take on things in my own strength. I thank you that even in my shortcomings there is no condemnation in you. Allow me to forgive myself fully as you have already done. When I fall, I pray that you would sustain me and remind me to get back up. My footsteps are ordered by you, and I thank you that you direct all my ways in your love, joy and peace. Continue to do as you have always done by placing me back safely on solid ground. Amen.

Scripture

2 Corinthians 12:9
Romans 8:1
Psalm 136
Colossians 1:4
Psalms 103:12

Personal Reflection

Is the company that you keep encouraging you to get up when you fall?

_____

_____

_____

_____

_____

What new adventures are your fears holding you back from?

_____

_____

_____

_____

Whose map are you allowing to lead your way?

_____

_____

_____

_____

Thoughts

_____
_____
_____
_____
_____
_____
_____
_____
_____
_____
_____
_____
_____
_____
_____
_____
_____
_____
_____
_____
_____
_____
_____

Encounter Two: Checking The Bags

One Wednesday night, I was at church. I was asked to get a poster board and write something that I have battled and overcome. The request was simple enough, so I obliged. I wrote "NOT UGLY." I was so proud of my beautiful penmanship and ability to write this out flawlessly in a straight line.

Excited to share a little piece of my life and a beautiful piece of art, I found that this seemingly easy project needed some clarification from the others who were presenting. After the much needed instruction, my team leader exclaimed; "I want you to use both sides of the poster board. One side will reflect the issue or challenge that you have faced. On the other side please write the victory."

I retrieved my board and began to write, "B-E-A-U", but I couldn't finish. In that moment, I felt immobilized. It was as if my Sharpie had been overtaken. All I could think was, "Wait. Am I spelling something wrong? Is my board not straight? What is it?" Something just did not feel right.

"That's not it, Lahoma," I heard. I felt a tug deep in my heart, a sense of uneasiness. As I stretched my hand out to continue with this seemingly easy project, I felt it again. I know I haven't always thought I was beautiful. I felt something like this before, but what was it?

Maybe it was something I ate. "Lord, what am I missing? What do I write?" And as clear as day, I felt I heard to word REJECTED!

Rejected? I have had some obstacles and challenges in my life, but rejection was something that I definitely have not battled. I had the sharpie in one hand and the board in the other. I tried to figure out what on earth was happening. I thought "God, what? I am not a reject!" But I lost the battle because God knew me better than I knew myself. What could it hurt? After all, in a church of this magnitude, surely someone else needed this.

As I began to hunt for a new board, my team leader was puzzled as to why someone would destroy such a masterpiece; after all, it was a perfectly fine board. Her glimpse of my initial, internal conflict probably perplexed her enough not to ask any questions.

We arrived early on the following Wednesday, and I went on a hunt for my old board. After all, this was truly what I was supposed to be sharing. My team leader was so caught up with what the rest of the group was doing that I could not get her attention to locate the old board.

This overwhelming sense of indescribable fear came over me as I was about to get on stage. Many questions flooded my mind as I took the long walk to my position marked on the floor. All I could think of was running, but it was already too late. I'm a half step from my position. Walking with my head down, I felt naked as if only this cheap board was all that covered me.

REJECTED. I felt I was on stage for hours, but it really translated into about four seconds. Swoosh. The speed of wind gushed as I flipped my poster board to reveal UNCONDITIONALLY LOVED. Full of anxiety, I didn't return to my usual seat, row five, column 2 north. In fact, I buried myself in the crowd. "Thank you God. I did what I feel like you wanted. Now, let's get on with it." I was hoping and praying that none of my peers just witnessed that process.

Charlotte Scanlon-Gambill from Hillsong gave the night's message about traveling. She overemphasized the good old days of air travel when everything was free, and you actually got a meal on the plane. She also mentioned having to strip down to go through security, and even the fact that the baggage didn't have to be weighed.

I know I am guilty of stuffing my bag to the max, crossing my fingers, and hoping that it isn't overweight. "Sometimes you get to the front and your bag is overweight; you have to take some of the things out because it is too heavy for the flight," she said. She then correlated that with our lives. It was so simple yet, profound. Sometimes in our lives we carry things that are too heavy, and we have to get rid of those things to get to our destination.

So many people talked to me about my board after service, and I was then in agreement with God. He knew what he was doing. Those people needed that. I stayed and spoke with many other women about their challenges. I asked them what they would write if they had a board. Exhausted from the busyness of the day, the anxiety of sharing something so heavy, and the conversations, I knew that the moment my face touched anything resembling a pillow, I would be out!

That's right. I would be in dreamland within a matter of minutes. I feel God speaks best to me in two places. One of those is the middle of worship, and the other is in my sleep. This particular night, I dreamt I was in this huge airport at the ticket counter.

Bags in hand, I approached the counter, a nice gentleman reached his hand out to assist me. He whispered in my ear, "The rejection that you have been carrying is too heavy for this flight." "What do you mean rejection?" I exclaimed loudly. "Ma'am, I need to get you on this flight, but I will need to get those bags," he said calmly and softly so that no one could hear our conversation.

I gently tossed my bag on the scale. "Ma'am, it weighs too much to travel," he said. "No sir, I said. "I have carried that from bag city to city for the last 9 years and not once has it ever been overweight." "Weigh it again because maybe the items on the inside haven't settled," I said.

"Still overweight," he said calmly. I was so irritated at this point that I broke down. The tapping of my bag handle moved to a violent slam, over and over, on the top of this bag. "With all that I have going on in my life right now, I don't need one more thing," I said under my breath. I quickly threw the bag back on the scale and said, "Here, just check my bags." Then he said, "Is there anything we can take out? We are just a few pounds away from where we need to be."

I ripped open the top zipper with the thought to take out whatever was on top. I grabbed a heavy rock. It was the kind of rock that some people have all over their yards. This rock in my bag had the word REJECTION etched on it, mid-center. I didn't know it was even in my bag. I guess it slipped in, but how and why was it there? "I don't have time," I said. I zipped my bag up and put it back on the scale to find out that it was so much lighter, and I even had room to spare.

Being the gentleman that he was, he said, "Ma'am, you can now move through security and board the plane." As I wiped the residue of tears from my eyes, I walk though security to board my plane. In the seat, with my tray table in its upright position, I put my carry-on in the overhead compartment and my purse underneath the seat in front of me. I reached down for my seat belt; I fastened it tight and prepared for takeoff.

The pilot warned that the flight would be short but turbulent, so the "fasten seat belt" sign would not go off. The pilot said, "Only move if you have to; the flight attendants are here to help you with anything that you may need." So we're off. I still had the sniffles, which were the evidence that I had been crying. But as we took off, everything seemed fine. After all, I wasn't an amateur.

We reached the expected altitude, and we were coasting. I could see the once huge buildings begin to look like small trees as I leaned forward to peer through the window of the lady on my right. Down the aisle way, I saw a man walking; it was the strangest thing because it was my dad, or at least I thought it was. "Dad, is that you? What are you doing here? I didn't know you were coming." He looks at me, but something weird happened.

I looked down at my hands to see them shrink before my eyes. "Wait, what's going on with me?" I think. It was as if I were morphing into a little girl. Not just any little girl, but the one on the side of the couch that held onto her dad's neck, begging him not to go. I was the little girl promising to be good and to always do what he wanted. "I promise, just stay! I won't do anything wrong. Don't leave," I said. The flashback felt so real. I even felt my mom's hands pry me loose from his neck. And in an instant, he was gone. I began to cry out "NO!"

With tears rolling down my cheeks, I saw a flight attendant

reach out to hand me a tissue. As I took it and dried my eyes, I saw my baby sister in her arms! I started rubbing my eyes because, surely, this was not happening to me. I looked again and saw that it wasn't a flight attendant, but my aunt! But this time, I noticed that I was older, about thirteen. I looked down to discover my favorite pair of short shorts. "What is going on?" I'm thinking. My aunt comes, stands in front of me, and looks me square in the eyes.

It was like she was mad at me. Tears welled up again and before I could say I was sorry, I hear, "We don't need you; we have our little girl now. Go on with your stuck up self miss bossy." Those were the same words spoken to me as a thirteen year old girl when my step mom had my baby sister. "LET ME OFF! I want off this plane," I screamed. The pain in my heart became unbearable. It was as if I was that little girl all over again. Then in an instant, she was gone. Afraid of what was going on, I pushed the button to call the flight attendant in hopes that somehow, someway, I could get off of that plane!

A new flight attendant arrived and her approach was pretty shaky because the turbulence in the air was rough. Swaying back and forth, she finally arrived at my seat. "Ma'am, wait. I'm sorry, sir, can you please..." While she was talking, I looked up and said, "Jason, what are you doing here? You were my first 'real' boyfriend." He opened his mouth and these words came rushing out like a flood: "You are so ugly; no one will ever love you. You are lucky to be with a boy like me. You shouldn't care what I do! You're lucky that anyone will put up with you. I am all that you have. You aren't worth anything. You're poor and even your daddy didn't want you."

I wanted out! I felt as if a thousand knives pierced my heart, but it was done in a way that I could feel every bit of pain. "God, why are these people all around me, and why do I have to be here?" I unbuckled my seat belt, jumped up and tried to run away!

I ran as best as I could down the aisle and a hand reached out to help me stand up straight. There was so much turbulence! He looked up and said, "The line for the bathroom is long so you might want to sit back down. It's not safe to be standing because at any minute, we may hit an air pocket." I say, "I'm not looking for the bathroom! I'm looking for the exit door!"

"The pilot can't stop, and we are almost there. I'll help you walk back to your seat," the man said. He walked me back to my seat and with tears in my eyes, I sat down. It was hard to breathe. I was crying so hard that everything hurt as I buckled in.

On this flight, each passenger had their own TV screen, and suddenly they all turned on. Displayed on each screen, seen by every passenger on the plane, was a scene from an encounter during college. I saw myself asking him, "How can you have sex with me and not even kiss me?" As the volume increased to the highest treble. A loud chuckle proceeded from his mouth followed by his smooth voice saying, "Kissing means something, and I don't want you to think I have feelings for you. I came here for one reason and one reason only. Lahoma, no one wants you. My friends and I had a bet on who could get you first, and I won. After all, I have a baby on the way."

Suddenly, masks shot down from the cabin ceiling as the pressure changed; no one could breathe. I wondered whether or not I should put the mask over my face. At this point, there was no reason to breathe. I was going to get off the plane one way or another. As I let my mask dangle from the ceiling, I blacked out for a moment. I came back to my senses, and within a few seconds, I began to breathe again.

The turbulence subsided as we approached our landing site. The plane made additional circles. The pilot explained that the flight traffic required us to re-approach the landing area. Flight attendants quickly scurried by to ensure that everyone was buckled in safely. I just left my head down because the thought of anything else happening was intolerable.

A man, who I thought was going to walk past me, abruptly stopped and stood before me. My eyes were so red and my tears so heavy that all I could make out was a white suit. Wait. I could tell that the suit used to be white, but was drenched in fresh, red blood. As my eyes started to focus, the red started to fade back into a crisp white. The white suit began to get brighter and brighter.

He reached for my hand, and he walked me backwards from the door. With no hesitation, I quickly lunged up and attempted to get past him and get off. I couldn't take anything else happening; I had to get off. He was a strange looking man; I could tell that he had something behind his back.

Surprisingly, he was strong, and my lunge didn't affect him one bit. He actually stood so strong that he sent me back a few steps. In tears, I pulled down my belongings from the overhead compartment. Finally, I saw what is behind him. It was the tail of his tuxedo! My vision was still blurry, but I noticed he had on a tux, not a suit. The tail of his tux was the same length as the train on a wedding gown. I dropped my bags. I was so perplexed and angry at this point that I just stood still staring at him. He then took the tail of his tux and covered me.

I thought that he did this because of the video that everyone saw, so I just allowed myself to be hidden in this seemingly never-ending train. He wrapped me in his train like a newborn baby. After wrapping me, he then lifted me and tucked me close to his chest where I began to wail and scream. There was such comfort in his arms; I was hidden from the shame, hurt, and rejection. I just stayed in his arms, lying on his chest. He held me, and I knew that I was safe and that he was not going to drop me. He held me so close.

As I begin to calm down, I heard him whisper, "Unconditionally loved." He repeated this over and over. Then he said, "I am sorry my daughter. I had to take you there so that I could show you where I have brought you from and what I have delivered you out of. Again and again, he whispered, "Unconditionally loved." The more he said it, the tighter I held on. I needed him to tell me that repeatedly after all I had experienced on the flight. I felt like something in my spirit broke. It was as if HE had truly taken the pain away. The morning alarm startled me as I looked around to see where I was. I was in the middle of my bed in the fetal position with tears rolling down my cheeks.

I had a rough night, to say the least! I then began to pray. I refused to move from my spot in the fetal position until I got some clarity and understanding. That flight revealed those deep hidden things that I had played off as if they were nothing. While I prayed, all I heard in my head over and over were the words unconditionally loved.

As the day went on, I stayed in the same position in the middle of my bed. I began to recount all aspects of this dream; I realized that every part was significant.

From check-in to the landing, it all had to mean something. As I prayed and pondered these thoughts, I kept hearing the words unconditionally loved.

Those things revealed were so heavy and so deep in my heart, and I had no idea that I lived out of this place of heaviness. Areas in my life were weighed down and He, Jesus, saw that I was finally in a place where I was ready to be shown what it was that I had been holding onto.

This process hurt. Reliving those instances, even in a dream, was painful. I was hurt; I felt betrayed, wounded, and abandoned all over again. REJECTION. Yes, that word was for me, not someone else.

As I lay in bed, I received a revelation. The seat belt that kept me buckled in was his grace, which kept me in position, even in the midst of everything. The bag was weighed down with hurt and rejection. The oxygen that re-entered me was the Holy Spirit giving me the air that I needed to live this life. The people that I encountered on the flight were those I needed to forgive because the hurt was still so deep.

The man in white was Jesus, and He picked me up and put me in His strong and mighty arms. Jesus was not moved or shaken when I ran or failed. The blood represented the covenant that once and for all forgave me and washed me clean. The plane's altitude represented the next level He was bringing me to.

There is a plane ride that we all must take. Although the turbulence exists, buckle up! It will not last long, and Jesus will wrap you in his robe of righteousness. As for me, the tears dried and the uncovered wounds were made whole. He promises to do the same for you, if you let Him.

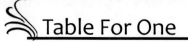

Prayer

Lord, I pray that you take me on the plane ride to heal those areas where you desire to bring wholeness. God as my comfort, when turbulence arises, I ask that you would set the course straight. Your word says that you comfort us in all our troubles so that we can comfort those in any trouble with the comfort we ourselves have received from you. God, thank you for comfort. I thank you that I am no longer a slave to sin, rejection, and shame because you have set me free. You know what is best for me, and you meet me right where I am. I pray for the strength and courage to confront those areas of hurt and pain in my life. Thank you that you are my advocate. God, I thank you that you are not the source of my hurt and pain. You mourn with me when I morn. You are the source of my life, freedom and restoration. I put my hope and trust in your unconditional love for me. At this moment, God, wrap me in your arms where I am safe and secure. Thank you God that your word says in Matthew 11:30 that Your yoke is easy to bear, and the burden You give me is light. Take the burdens that I have been carrying and bring forth healing, wholeness and freedom. Thank you Lord. Amen.

Scripture

Matthew 6:5-15
Matthew 11:30
2 Corinthians 2:4
Leviticus 19:18

Personal Reflection

Reflect on what your plane ride would look like? Who would be the people that would appear for you? What steps will you take to forgive those people?

_____
_____
_____
_____
_____

When you experience turbulence, what is your comfort?

_____
_____
_____
_____
_____

Have you ever felt like you have overcome something, but still find yourself struggling? Explain.

_____
_____
_____
_____
_____

When was the last time you checked your bags?

_____
_____
_____
_____
_____

Thoughts

Encounter Two: Checking The Bags

Encounter Three:
The Dress

*W*alking into this trendy new store in Austin, TX, making my typical b-line to the clearance rack, I was inadvertently distracted. Out the corner of my eye, I spotted a beautiful dress. This dress was stylish and classic; it was screaming to be on my body! It included everything I would ever want in an article of clothing: beauty, high quality and uniqueness. I had to try this dress on! Cautiously, I approach the rack and, to my amazement, I found one my size. I snatched the dress off the rack and proceeded immediately to the dressing room. I could feel the soft fabric gliding across my skin and the tinge of the cold zipper as I zipped the back of the dress up.

Barefoot in the dressing room, I began twirling like a princess in front of the massive oversized vintage mirror. I felt beautiful in this dress like a new woman. I took my time looking at the dress from all angles. My "girls" were perfectly accentuated, yet not over emphasized. My less desirable "trunk" area smooth and my waist looked like a coke bottle. Planted in front of the mirror for quite some time, I fantasized about all the great places I could go in that dress.

The dress had everything I could have ever asked for, but where was the price? Gazing at myself in the mirror, I realized I had not even considered the price. Slowly, re-entering the dressing room, I removed my dress in hopes of finding a price tag price low enough to indulge in this great find. My glance at the glossy tag proved that this designer was very proud of this dress. Contemplating the hefty price, I felt that it was well worth it. Under old circumstances, I would have given in, but it was far outside my budget at the time. I decided to operate with some level of self control, but believe me, I was going to have that dress.

I did not let money keep me from going back to the store and trying the dress on over and over again. I called the store often thinking perhaps it would eventually go on sale. Every call, no matter which employee, I heard the same story, "We do not have special sales or offer discounts. We understand the quality and value of the items that we carry. We offer high quality products and our policy has stood the test of time. They are worth what we are asking for and more."

Saving every free penny in an effort to get this extremely expensive, but valuable dress was worth it because I realized this dress was my dress. Arriving home late from hours of extra over-time, I was shocked at the contents in my mailbox. It was a refund check from an over payment of state taxes. Confirmation that this was my dress! Anxiety coupled with joy caused me to toss and turn all night. I could barely sleep thinking about my dress. I knew exactly where my dress was located in the store, and the idea of finally being able to go all of the places I dreamt up kept me wide awake.

After departing from work that evening, I headed directly to the store, and there it was! Just as I envisioned, the dress was there. Removing it gently from the rack and pulling it in towards me, I glided my hand across the dress to again feel the fabric and catch a whiff of the black-cherry vanilla store scent woven deep into the rich fabric.

Approaching the sales counter, I heard, "An exquisite choice." The saleswoman validated my purchase decision. Laying the dress on the counter gave me an unexplainable sense of value and satisfaction; she hung my dress on the rack to prepare it for the garment bag. I stared at my dress; it looked a little smaller than I remembered. To my surprise, this dress was the wrong size. I got so caught up in the moment; I assumed that this was the one in my size. "Ugh!" I exclaimed dastardly. Her head tilted, eyebrows wrinkled, as she shrugged questioning what happened. In an extremely irrational tone, I shrieked, "Where is my dress?".

I began to explain all the things leading up to that point. For instance, the last few weeks and months I have been regularly admiring this dress, the fact that it fit like a glove, the even sadder fact that I told all my friends, and saved money. I told her that in my waiting for this dress, I received an unexpected check in the mail which allowed me to come back sooner than expected. Desperately, I pleaded for her to tell me that she had my dress. Emotionally charged by my story and reaction, she frantically looked through the system to make sure they didn't have any more in my correct size. Her eyes glossy with a profound look of disappointment, "We do not have any more here in the store," she says.

"This cannot be happening to me; this dress is mine I exclaim! There must be something that you can do. Who is your manager? Who is in charge? Better yet, who is the designer? Can I order the dress directly?" Sensing my desperation and entangled in my emotional distress, she checked the computer to see if any other stores had it in the region.

On the verge of tears as she searched, she inhaled deeply and followed it with a heartfelt smile, "We have only one left in the region, and it is in the store located over two hours away, but I can have it shipped here just for you." Prepared in this moment to drive for hours to get my dress, I considered the time of night. By the time I arrived, the store would be closed.

Obliged that it could be shipped within a matter of days, I waited. It felt like a lifetime, but I had already waited this long, a few more days would not hurt. Two days passed and the dress arrived as promised! Dress in one hand, cell phone in the other, I excitedly shared the news. I reached down to call my best friend and found this text message blaring at me:

> *"You have amazing strengths. You deal with stress & carry heavy burdens; You smile when you feel like screaming. You sing when you feel like crying. You cry when you are happy & laugh when you are afraid; your love is unconditional. There's only 1 thing wrong, you forget your worth!"*

Nothing is coincidental. Even this moment with this text message in one hand and dress in the other, my thoughts were immediately sent into a tailspin. Correlating this situation to where I was in my life, I began taking stock and re-evaluating my value. This dress was valuable to me. It came at a very high price, and I was willing to go through great lengths to get it. If the dress were on sale, I would have most certainly taken the reduced price. Still I question the effort and great lengths I would have gone through if it were on sale.

I waited on this dress, thought about it often, shared the news with friends and God unexpectedly made a way by providing a refund just at the right time. The store had to ship it specifically for me. I acknowledged that I have not considered value in this way before. This dress was just like my life, only in reverse, especially when it came to men. Unlike the dress, I discounted myself. As a matter of fact, at times, I asked for a low price and then negotiated an even lower price. The dress, which was worth a lot, did not come at a discount. This helped to keep the perceived value intact. It could have just as easily been 30, 50 or 80 percent off, but it wasn't. It was full price, and the store understood the value.

I got home with thoughts raging like the seas, happy about my dress purchase, but heavy with "If I valued me, how could I..." statements. Statements like, "If I valued me, how could I give a man the time of day who could care less if he spent time with me, or hang after the club with a man knowing his intentions at almost a quarter to three in the morning?" "If I valued me, how could I entertain connecting my soul with a man without even the faintest desire to have a relationship with God or talk on the phone for hours and be intimate with a married man?" "If I valued me, how could I really meet a guy and invite him in my home knowing nothing about him?"

Thoughts and flowing questions grew out of the wood works of my brain; the simple answer was "I couldn't and I wouldn't." Fear shook me. I wondered if men, or people in general didn't see my value. Who says that I am worth more than this? Even with the fear of setting a higher price in this moment with all the fleeting thoughts, I made a decision to no longer sell myself at a discount.

I picked up my journal and started to write, I wrote down situations that I could remember where I sold myself short. This process felt hopeless because I began to write page after page in my journal. I could not even think of a single time where I actually valued myself. Remorseful and repentant, the Lord just began to settle my heart about my value. I realized that my emotions wanted to take control and validate the fact that I felt worthless, but there was this sense deep in me that this could not be true. I began to look up every scripture that I could find about what the lord says about me:

> I am loved by God, Jhn 3:16. Forgiven, Col. 1:14. Saved by grace through faith, Eph. 2:8. Called with a Holy calling, 2 Tim 1:9. Created in his image, Rom 8:29. Complete in Him, Col 2:10. More than a conqueror, Rom. 8:37. Not moved by what I see, Rom 4:19. The elect of God, Col 3:12. Predestined to be conformed to His image, Rom. 8:29. Letting his truth set me free, Jhn 8:32,36.

During this time, I received a huge revelation. There were many people who would have loved the dress, but because they were unwilling to pay the price, they could not have it. Some people walked past the dress because they didn't perceive the value, but the right person knew. People tried it on and found that it was not a good fit or it didn't match the recently purchased shoes, but the dress still did not diminish in value. Regardless of recognition, the value never changed. The dress didn't have a complex because its value wasn't recognized, it had a price and either someone had it or they did not.

I began to write these verses on index cards all over the house and in random places. I armed myself with a script, similar to the one that the store employees read me every time someone asked about a sale or discount. "We don't have sales or special discounts; we offer high quality products and our policy stands because we understand what these items are worth." The new script had to replace the old one. After all it had been on repeat way too long. I had to repeat it over and over and still do to make sure that the exchange takes place from my head to my heart. Then and only then have I been on this journey of value discovery, healthy boundaries and a strong sense to just wait on God's best. The dress was not anxious about anything. I went after what I wanted, and I believe that whomever God has for me will do the same.

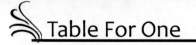

Prayer

*T*hank you that you call me valuable, righteous, holy, and worthy. God, I thank you for a fresh revelation of my worth and the price that you have paid. Thank you that I do not have to be anxious about anything because I can come to you and ask anything in your name. Open my mind and heart, search every part of me and show me where I have sold myself short. As you reveal these things to me also show me your infinite love and grace that cover me. Give me wisdom and insight to enlighten my understanding of my value and worth. Thank you that you for not putting new wine in old wineskins but instead making my value and worth brand new. Amen.

Scripture

Ephesians 2
1 Corinthians 6:20
1 Corinthians 7: 23

Personal Reflection

What is the price you have been asking for your "dress"?

_____

_____

_____

_____

_____

Do you value things that you get at a discount the same way you do when you purchase them at full price? Explain.

_____

_____

_____

_____

_____

What are some things that you keep at the forefront of your mind in terms of not settling or compromising for less than what you are worth?

_____

_____

_____

_____

_____

What are some of your "If I valued me…" statements?

_____

_____

_____

_____

_____

Thoughts

Encounter Four:
Field of Flowers

*E*veryone needs a relaxing day. You know, where there's not a whole lot going on, listening to your favorite songs, debating on doing laundry, screening phone calls while rejecting those calls that are one-sided. Enjoying my relaxing day, my closest guy friend, Derrek, calls. Derrek, being a smooth, predictable, non-emotional creature made it an easy choice to engage in conversation, even on a relaxed day. "Hey, D!" To my surprise, a loud voice on the other end belts out, "We are going to do this!" "That's awesome, so happy for you," all the while thinking that I clearly missed something. My tone resembled something like "do what and why are you yelling?" After all, this was totally out of character for him. "I am going to ask her to marry me!" I screamed so loud and became so overwhelmed with excitement; you would have thought he was asking me!

The richness of joy and love felt in this moment ran so deep, but in an instant it turned cold and stark. It was as if the hues of red and violet turned to a dark dingy grey, not with the happy couple, but deep in my heart. I was sincerely happy for them, or I wanted to be, at least. They are great together, good for each other, and committed to loving one another. After a split second of joy, sadness overtook me.

What about me God? Do I not deserve to be loved? What does she have that makes her lovable that I do not have? Am I not a gift? I rode down pity party lane; the longer I asked questions, the more questions came like a flood, fleeting thought after fleeting thought. It brought me to a point of being overwhelmed and consumed with tears. It broke my heart so hard and so deep; it was hard to breath. I lay prostrate on the floor telling myself, get up, dust yourself off. As the overwhelming thoughts began to break, I felt like I heard the Lord speak softly to my heart, "I want to be your husband."

In anguish and devastation with a great sense of unworthiness, I began to weep all over again. It went on for what felt like hours. Angrily I screamed, "God, I do not want you to be my husband." Recognizing the manner in which God speaks to me, I heard again, "I want to be your husband." These words made me even more angry and mad. I thought, that's just like God to say something like that as though he could really be my husband. As a matter of fact, if he cared, he would take the desire away, so I wouldn't have to deal with the tears and the yearnings that he placed in my heart to begin with.

As I lifted my sobbing body off the ground, I began to fantasize about what a real husband would be like. Late night pillow talks, a dozen red roses with a few yellow sunflowers, intimacy, sweet notes and poems in random places to be discovered, and even sweet little kisses every now and again for no reason. Wallowing in my funk, thinking on all that I want and deserve, I felt as if God opened the door to my patio and asked me to step outside. Oddly and angrily enough, I went on the patio for air to pull myself back together. All the while thinking that no matter if I get it together outside, I will return to my empty house with my empty bed and empty seat on the other side of the table.

Flop, the sound made as I leaned in on the rail, "What do you see?" "God, please stop, just stop," I yelled loudly. Exasperated, gritting my teeth, I mustered up the reply, "You made everything that I see, and you know what I am looking at." "What do you see?" I exhale deeply in disgust. "I see the back of an apartment building directly behind me. I see a field of green grass to my right with some flowers in the same proximity and a bike on a patio be low." "What do you see?" Even angrier than I was before: building, grass, flowers, bike. Ugh.

"Look again, this time just focus on those flowers that you see over by the grass. My daughter, you want a husband that will bring you a dozen roses, but I have given you the field." Gulp. My head dropped like a heavy weight rested on my neck; a lump formed in my throat as though I just swallowed a huge rock that wouldn't go down. Nothing could be done to hold back the tears as I stood motionless looking over the balcony gazing at the field of flowers that he made just for me.

As I wept in this seemingly out of body experience, I felt such great pain. I have been searching all this time for completion in a husband when I have not fully loved the one that I already have. A sense of strong conviction rose as a result of knowing that I had been stuck in this place so long. I didn't realize that God wanted to be my husband. In my remorseful state, I began to ask God to forgive me for the many times that I haven't allowed him to be my mate, to forgive me for my responses as though he owed me something. He loved me, and He gave me the freedom to choose and now, I chose him. I wanted him to romance me and show me the many ways he is present and available. He opened my eyes to see him in ways that I could see, feel and understand.

I wanted to share this encounter with you to remind you that God cares about every detail of your life, and he tells us that we have not because we ask not. I want to encourage you to ask! Ask God to show you his thoughts towards you! Ask him to romance you and you will be amazed at all the things that he does to love, romance, care and listen to you. Ask him to show you his character, and who he is!

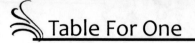

Prayer

*G*od, I thank you that you are mindful of me. Seal the essence of this chapter in my heart that I may begin to understand how wide, how deep and how great your love is for me. Thank you that you shift my focus from the things that I do not possess to those things which you have given me. Make me aware of the field that I may harvest from. Lord, be my delight and show me more of who you are. I receive your love, romance and affection. God, reveal to me the tangible affection that you have for me. Amen

Scripture

Ephesians 3:20
Psalms 8:4
Romans 4:21
Luke 18:3-5
Psalms 37:4

Personal Reflection

How are you allowing God to be your spouse?

_____

_____

_____

_____

_____

What are your responses when someone else finds the mate of their dreams? Why?

_____

_____

_____

_____

_____

What desires have you placed in God's hands?

_____

_____

_____

_____

Thoughts

Encounter Five:
Pregnant

*I*mmediately overwhelmed by the news of my pregnancy, I begin working on a strategic plan with one action item, RUN! Run from everything and everyone, step down from church leadership, re-assign my ministry roles and transfer my job. I cannot face everyone with news like this. In an instant, I completed a road map for my exit strategy, down to playing out each hard conversation repeatedly in my head. I thought, I can run to a place where no one knows me. Simple strategy, lace up the Nikes, run! Immediate execution of the plan left a cushion for any hiccups or delays. The execution began flawlessly without a single red flag. Strangely enough, even in my disappointment, I would often find myself jaunting past mirrors in the house to raise my shirt exposing my once much flatter belly. Although there was not much joy in these glimpses, I periodically checked to see if it was real. In denial as to how I even got to this place that has cost me everything, my remorseful heart considered the pain, disappointment and hurt this would cause those who look up to me; I remained silent about it all.

When I finally reached a place where I could wake up in the morning feeling normal, a knock at the front door startled me; this is very unusual. I glanced at the clock before inquiring who it was at the door to make sure that it was really 7am. To my surprise, my best friend, Andrea, was at the door. Inviting her in, I could sense something was on her mind. She looked me square in my eyes. "I know this sounds crazy, but I have been praying for you over the last few months harder than ever, and I could not shake the feeling that I was supposed to come see you this morning, so here I am. " Extreme terror eked through every inch of my body as though someone kicked me so hard in the chest that the wind was knocked out of me. A blank cold stare deep in her eyes was followed by a shallow smile and a casual brush off. "Girl, that is so strange." My heart palpitated with a fire of tears rising on the inside as I continued to deflect this conversation. "I do not know what that is all about, but I am good. Thanks for listening and obeying what you felt like was Jesus. I appreciate it, but I am so good."

Breaking down at this point would cause my plan to fall apart, and I just could not let that happen. Andrea takes a shallow breath and sighs with a deep release, "I'm so glad because for some reason in my dreams, I kept seeing you hold a baby. It was the strangest thing." Please! Are you kidding? She turned her body back in the direction of the front door. Come on now! Golden silence embodied my apartment for what seemed like hours as she made her approach towards the door.

I truly began to consider the consequences of my choices. I began to discover that my grand plan came at a massive cost. Andrea is perceptive but not a pusher, so she just took what I said with confidence, probably thinking that maybe she was the one a little off. I knew better. Imagining her thoughts tore me up on the inside, still unwilling to expose my faults and this huge awful selfish plan. As she walked away, I exuded a sense of reassurance towards her as if I were being honest with her. So much so that I began to believe all the nonsense myself. As she headed out for work, I could sense her uneasy, yet joyful confusion.

As I began getting ready for work, I could feel a heavy clinching weight in my heart. It was numb and listless; I looked aimlessly for my other shoe. Retracing my steps, I remembered the kitchen, front door, guest bed, and the master bath. I found it in my closet to the right under the shirts in the back. I must have thrown it off in a hurry to get to the restroom. Reaching down, I found something that I was definitely not looking for, my Breaking Point. Hiding this huge let-down with thoughts of disappointment, failure, rejection, condemnation and a sense of unworthiness took a hold of me like I have never felt before. Remorseful feelings were followed by a fountain of heavy warm, painful tears. My conscience got the best of me; I allowed a big mistake, in my eyes, to reshape my entire world.

Too terrified to face my choices, imagining the tears and pain made it easier to quickly overcome remorse. After all, they would have likely received me if I did not hide or run, but I reasoned that this hole was so deep that I must keep it together, lace my shoes tighter and run faster and harder. I mustered the courage to pull it together. After all, I cannot break; I must keep running!

"Beep, beep, beep. Beep, beep, beep," echoes loudly in my head. With a racing heart and sweaty palms, I reached up to gain mobility and the noise still danced in my head. Peering out of the closet in hopes of discovering where this awful beeping sound came from, I flipped over and opened both eyes to see 6:15 am flashing. This awful noise was my alarm clock. I bolted from under the covers and ran to the mirror to see if this was real. I glanced at myself and discovered that the whole thing really was a dream. It couldn't be; this all felt so real.

I could not shake the feeling; I rubbed my sweaty hands together. My heart beat like a drum in my head. Sprinting and tearing through the house, I searched for remnants of what felt so real, only to hear, "What you are looking for is not there." Although it is not the way I would like my story to unfold, it felt so real.

I disappointedly got ready for work as usual, calling Andrea to verify that she was not there; I just needed to know. I told her detail by detail of what happened, and she assured me that it was in fact a dream. I begged for her help in this moment because this was the realest dream I ever experienced. Sternly asking her to pray for me and just be there because I knew in my heart something was going on! "Lahoma, I am happy to be here and pray, but I think that only the Lord can uncover what your dream meant." Her response dropped heavily in my confusingly heart-wrenching moment. She needed to say more; I wanted her to walk me through this one and tell me exactly what to do. Instead, seeking God was the best advice she could give.

Angrily, I shrugged her words off, but after a little while, with no other alternatives, I did just that. I asked God what it all meant. Why pregnancy? Why Andrea? Why would I have run, hide and lie like that? What is happening to me? The audible response that I was looking for did not come, but I kept asking. This experience felt so real; I was not going to let it go without answers. I considered that maybe my husband was on the way or it was time for me to adopt or become a foster parent like I always wanted to do.

Desiring to properly discern God's voice, by faith, I began fasting, believing that he would reveal this mystery. Eventually, he began to show me with clarity. Pregnancy because He had put a vision on the inside of me that He was about to birth. Like a mother who is pregnant, He was preparing something great on the inside of me. I understood it would take time to be nurtured and grow and that things were changing and moving although I may not always visibly see what He was knitting together on the inside. He told me, "I am working in you, setting "Andreas" up all around you to help support the vision I will birth from your wound." The shoes were a sign that He was preparing me to run this race. "I am beginning to strengthen areas in you; when you run this time you will find refuge in me."

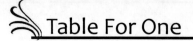

Prayer

*Y*our word reminds me that you are faithful to complete the work that you began in my life. I thank you that you knew me before I was formed and you called, predestined, justified and glorified me. I thank you that you teach me to run towards that which you called me to before the foundation of the earth. God I thank you that you are for me and since you are for me it does not matter who is against me. I put my confidence in you for the results that stem from the calling on my life. I lay down all my fears, my past and my future and offer you my present. Take me, right now, just as I am and use me for your purposes. Develop an awareness of the purpose for which you created me and a conviction to allow you to complete it. I pray for open doors, favor and authority. I will obey and trust you to bring the laborers to partner with me on this journey towards fulfilling my purpose. Amen

Scripture

Philippians 1:6
2 Timothy 4:7
Romans 8:28-31
Hebrews 12: 1-3
Jeremiah 29:11

Personal Reflection

What do you feel that God designed you to do specifically? Explain.

_____

_____

_____

_____

Do you ever feel like it is too late for you? Explain.

_____

_____

_____

_____

Is there a situation that you ran from before? Explain.

_____

_____

_____

_____

When you don't get your answer right away, what are the next steps that you take?

_____

_____

_____

_____

What race do you think God is preparing for you to run?

_____

_____

_____

_____

Thoughts

Encounter Six:
360

*T*here is a highway in Austin, Texas called 360. This highway is especially close to my heart because, where I am from, we don't have anything like it! Plush greens, mature trees, distinctive flowers are surrounded by massive mountains on each side that are out of this world, offering some of the most amazing views of the city. There are places on 360 that people take nature walks to experience the mountain peeks and beautiful rippling lake that runs through it. Often, I take extra time when traveling 360 to climb a small part of one of the mountains to experience the beauty of the endless landscape, although my first journey on 360 was less than magical. On my first drive, I was on my way to a potluck for a church small group event when my cell phone battery flashed, indicating it was too low to use my GPS, what I live by . There was enough juice left to take me from my office in downtown Austin to Highway 183 North to get to 360, so before turning it on, I got as far as I could before I put in the address of my destination in hopes it would have enough life.

I drove a little while with no GPS navigating me turn by turn and no written directions, a first for me and a minor accomplishment. Approaching the exit, I made a left to get on 360, and powered up my GPS to lead me the rest of the way. It took my cell phone a while to calculate the route because the battery was on its last half bar and the area does not provide good reception. I drove quite some time before it calculated my route. Based on what I knew about the location of the potluck, I did not panic because I knew it would take me a while to get there. So, as my route calculated, I drove in the right slow lane with cars zooming past. What would I do if I didn't have GPS? Intrigued by the new scenery, I just kept going. After a little while, I got restless and turned the music up as I continued to wait on my phone to calculate my route.

I removed the battery from my phone hoping that it would reset and put me on the right course. After my phone reset itself, I decided to make a call to the hosts to find out if I was on the right course. With one quarter bar left, I needed them to answer quickly. I called the first number on the invite. Someone picked up the phone, and I could hear the chatter from all the people in the background plus someone belting out an off key note from what sounded like the start of karaoke. A girl answered, "Chad Stephens' phone." "Hi, I am headed to the potluck, and I am lost. Can you please help me?" "I am having trouble hearing you, let me go outside." She replied. As soon as I heard the door shut, I rushed out, "My phone is about to die, can you please tell me how to get where you are? I am on 360 and do not know the cross street, but there is a church with a huge stained glass window on my right. I just passed over a lake." "Great! You are headed the right way. Just keep straight, and when you get to FM2222, make a right. Then head down until you see a gas station, and make a left." She replied. "Thank you! I will call back again if I get lost." As soon as I hung up the phone, my cell phone died.

I continued on 360 for quite some time, and I found it very interesting that so many of the streets had the same name. They really do "Keep Austin Weird." Low on gas, I pulled over to re-fuel at a gas station and confirmed the directions she had given me. A call back to Chad's phone was out of the question at this point. I asked the clerk, and he confirmed that I was on the right track to get to my destination.

I drove about 30 more minutes before approaching 183 again. Stunned that there were two 183's as well, I just kept driving.

This time things began to look familiar as if I had already been here before. Thinking that it was deja vue, I continued driving. I glanced at my phone to see if perhaps I could attempt to power it back up for just one more call, but when it powered on, an error message displayed "too low for radio use," and it immediately powered back down. I began to get anxious because surely people would be leaving or someone has probably impolitely coughed or breathed on the food. I can take not socializing, but I cannot let go of my germophobic tendencies.

An hour into the drive made me regret even attempting this party, so I decided to go home and just forget the whole thing. After all, I would not be hungry because I brought enough mashed potatoes to feed a football team! I made up in my mind that at the next intersection, I would just turn around and go home. I could see the intersection at a distance and as I approached it, I saw the gas station that I got gas from not long ago.

I knew I had a long day, but come on, that was beyond strange. I got out of the car again to see if it was the same station or if it was just so similar that I thought I was headed the wrong way. I saw that the man at the counter was the same one who confirmed my directions earlier. "I'm back! I am not sure how I ended back up here, but somehow I did." He smiled, walked over to the maps on the turning display and pulled it out to help me better navigate. He started with, "You see, 360 is a loop. It is unlike any other place in Austin. Eventually you will see the same streets over and over again." All I could think was that he could have just as easily told me this the first time!

"Sir, if I want to get off 360 which way am I am supposed to go? I would like to get home, and I live on Wells Branch Parkway." He walked over to the printer in the back of the store, grabbed a clean sheet of paper and wrote out for me turn by turn what to do to get home. He taught me something unique about 360; it does not end. It just loops. I guessed I missed out on that number correlation thing, but I surely would not forget it now! I thanked him profusely and headed on my way. I was irrationally irritated and being at a potluck was probably not the best place to be anyway.

How dumb will people think that I am when I tell them that I went on a circular highway, and it was not until approximately

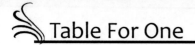

the seventh time around that someone pointed it out to me?! I wonder if it matters how dumb I think I look, or if it would be worse to live my life in this way? Not seeing the signs ahead and re-visiting the same areas, but the truth of the matter is, this is exactly where I was.

I would be on fire for God, attempt to walk it out alone, sin, fall hard, and go back over and over and over again. I think of the scripture Proverbs 26:11: "As a dog returns to his vomit, so a fool will return to his foolishness." At this point in my journey I was traveling on 360/ I kept going back to the places that he had freed me and delivered me from over and over. The place where there is no true progress, just circles. I was running in circles trying to earn God's approval, trying to please people and trying to gratify my flesh.

I became honest with myself because of 360, which is where I spent most of my life. Maybe you have been on 360, and maybe I have passed you up a couple times, especially knowing how long I was there. But know that you don't have to stay on 360. You can walk in all that God has called you to by asking him to show you what road you are on and recognizing the signs that guide you in the right direction. I want you to know that 360 is the easiest road, but you find yourself getting the same results, which, by definition, is insanity.

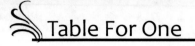

Prayer

*L*ord make me aware of the road in which I am traveling. Reveal those places that cause me to make the same mistakes repeatedly and stunt my growth in you. May you cause every area in my life to bear fruit that brings you glory. Take me to a new level of maturity in you as you order each one of my steps. You are my GPS; you are a trustworthy guide and I thank you that you position me and walk with me into all that you have for me. Help me to wander in circles, but live a life that is Spirit led. I declare new territory and old things are passed away. I am moving forward. Amen.

Scripture

Psalms 26:11
Proverbs 20:24
Psalms 119: 35, 133
Jeremiah 10:23

Personal Reflection

What areas of your life do you find yourself on 360?

_____

_____

_____

_____

_____

How often do you allow God to direct your steps?

_____

_____

_____

_____

_____

Provide an example of when you tried to self navigate a situation. What was the outcome?

_____

_____

_____

_____

_____

Thoughts

Encounter Seven:
Eviction

$\mathcal{O}$ut of breath and extremely frustrated from a long, rainy day, I reached the top of my stairs to my third floor apartment and, in the distance, noticed something on my door. My first thought was stupid restaurant menus again! A closer look revealed this was not a menu; it was a real note. Oddly, someone took extra effort to fold it and tape the note to the door. Loosely opening the note, the words EVICTION NOTICE blared at me! Not only was my rainy day long and frustrating, but being homeless takes the cake. Fearful that an eviction notice meant they may have already locked me out, I cautiously opened the door and entered my apartment. I made a quick run through to take inventory of the things in my apartment, locked the door back and make a mad dash to the leasing office.

The office, swarming with residents, required me to wait patiently. In line, I discreetly read the top of the notice in hopes that this was a mistake. The momentary look at the notice proved that it was properly addressed. "I assure you that I paid my rent. Can you please help me with this," I whispered to the apartment manager. I had the mistaken notion that she would match my tone, but she blurted loudly, "Let me see your eviction notice, so that I can look you up in the system!" Mentally unprepared for the embarrassment, I attempted to shut the door to her office as she even more loudly exclaimed, "We do not typically make mistakes. We have a new system. You have not paid your rent!"

On the verge of losing my cool, mulling over every curse word in the book as I held my tongue tightly so that none would slip, I passive aggressively grabbed the carbon copy check to prove that my rent was in fact paid. I made this month's rent payment! "A carbon copy duplicate of a check is not sufficient proof that you paid your rent, anyone can make a check out and never drop it off. We require a copy of a cleared check from your financial institution. Without it, I cannot do anything about this eviction notice." "I cannot lose my home! Especially when I know that I paid my rent," I yelled robustly. The word eviction wallowed in the back of my mind as she callously provided me with alternate payment options.

"Fine, I will pay it again even though I am sure that I paid it." She looked at me with a smirk, "We only take debit and credit cards since we are this far in the month." Contemplating holding off so that I can do my own research, the consequences of losing my apartment made me quickly whip out my debit card. She returned with a receipt in duplicate in hand and motioned for the next resident.

I returned to my apartment soaking wet from my slow gallop back from the office, preoccupied with the thought of mistakenly overlooking the rent. As soon as I arrived back at the apartment, I called the bank to confirm the check and reviewed my online banking transactions. No sign of this check to be found! Frustrated to the point of tears, I ripped the eviction notice to shreds.

I was still uneasy because making that type of mistake was unlike me. In an instant, the rain went from a gentle glaze to violent fit, making it easy to just get some rest. The morning sun emerged; I rushed over to flip open my computer. I logged into my online banking thinking perhaps I missed something. As suspected, two rental payment charges appeared on my account! Both the regular check and the debit card charge went through.

I make my way through the puddles to work calling the office repeatedly. Of course they would not answer! Instead of handling this matter by phone, with evidence in hand, I jumped in the car and zoomed over to the office on my lunch break.

The manager nodded for me to come to her office, this time shutting the door apologetically. Before I could even speak, rationally and calmly, she said, "The phones have been out all day because of the rain. We converted to a new payment acceptance system only to find that it is much worse that what we had before. The new system misallocated some checks received this month, and you happen to be one of few units affected by this." Looking intently in her eyes, I asked, "What are you going to do to fix it?" "I have been working all morning to rectify the situation. I will refund your debit transaction and take money off your next month's rent." Unappreciative of her kindness because of my offense from the previous day, I impolitely responded, "I guess that will have to do then! I slid my un-presented evidence back in my purse and headed back to work.

Still, this situation was a shake-up of sorts. Before this incident, I had not even considered the value of a place to stay. Ample time to contemplate in the rain, I began to think about areas of my life that I possibly needed to evict! It is not often that I take stock of what resides in the apartment of my heart and mind. Exploring the idea further by asking God to show me what things I may need to put on notice.

Unexpectedly, so many things that needed to be evicted came to my mind. Things that had taken up residence that I was not even aware of. An eviction was necessary! I started the eviction process right away, beginning with the more blatant areas then moving in towards the etchings, the areas that have been residing so long that they were hard to still see.

Abandoned was etched lightly on the roof as I thought about the day my dad, H, step-dad, J, and step-dad, Mister, went away as I fought hard to be a good little girl so that they would not leave me. Unworthy was stained in the carpet as I considered all my failures and mistakes. Seeing the word brought me to tears as I was reminded of the deep insecurity and lie that no one could love someone who has a past like me. Betrayer was faded in a frame as I thought of the many times I have disappointed people. Ugly was smeared on a mirror only to be seen when the steam from the shower revealed it as I considered the way I felt about my body. Filthy was taped to the side of the trash can as I recounted the number of men I had given myself to. Undeserving was faintly scribbled across the dust on the top of the magazine rack as I thought about how love should not even come looking for some-one like me. Too late flashed across the alarm clock as I tried to think about salvaging and repairing all the things I had done.

The things etched in my heart had to carefully be removed because they did not belong there. In my own strength, I tried to evict, but frequently the dust would resettle. Messages from church of God's unconditional love and acceptance begin to rain down on my complex and over these areas. The rains fell so heavy that the entire apartment flooded, caved in and had to be torn down. The old complex with all the etchings was destroyed!

My complex looked the same on the outside, but the inside was rebuilt. A new complex was erected, but on a more sturdy foundation, a foundation of truth, unconditional love and peace. God's love has made me new and all the former things have passed away. I began to embrace the truth that I am loved, undeservingly loved by God. I cannot earn it, and I cannot lose it.

Prayer

Thank you that your love is unfailing and I cannot loose. Take every filthy area of my life and wash me with the water of your word to make everything clean and new. Re-establish my foundation on your rock that does not change. Please allow the etchings that are not from you to be erased and begin reflecting what you say about me. Give me the strength to never look back and boldy move into the purpose that you have for me. Thank you for your unconditional love that is always brand new. Amen

Scripture

Colossians 2:6-7
Matthew 7:24-28
Psalms 89:14,26

Personal Reflection

What do the etchings in the home of your heart read? Explain.

_____

_____

_____

_____

_____

Does your foundation need to be re-erected?

_____

_____

_____

_____

_____

What are some things in your life that you may need to evict?

_____

_____

_____

_____

_____

Thoughts

Encounter Eight:
The Soup

Dinner, alone? Me? NEVER! I would not dare appear lonely nor do anything alone, but there was something that just made me feel like I was supposed to do this. I played it safe; I chose my favorite Italian restaurant for dinner. My lack of enthusiasm was completely apparent as I maneuvered to the hostess stand that evening. The hostess politely explained that there was a wait because of prom and the entire restaurant was busy, but she offered me her last seat at the bar.

Negotiating every angle in my head; I opted for the bar seat. Maybe GOD knew that a table was too much for me right now. It was perfect! After all, I might be able to strike up a decent conversation with someone. Having dinner alone at the bar did not seem as daunting of a task as having a full table. The bar provided some security, many customers at the bar looked like they may have already had a few cold ones. In fact, I am probably looking rather lovely to them right now.

My bartender was handsome; he had an irresistible pearly white smile with smooth supple brown skin, all of which I picked up on in a matter of seconds when he gave me the "I will be right there" smile and nod. Yes God! While I patiently waited on my future prince, I fantasized about the way he would propose, our fam ily photos and our fabulous wedding day. As he approached, my palms got sweaty as I thought to myself, can I just call you my husband? "Girrrlfriend, what can I get fa you today?" Complete with two snaps and a shake on the end. Abruptly, my fantasy came to an end!

"I'll have water to drink," I grumbled as I laid down my fanatical love story with this man. I would like to go ahead and order as well, "Girl, I know that's right, a woman who knows what she wants. Girls like us have to stick together." It was all too much. Smile or cry, smile or cry? "Ha ha ha," I blurted loudly as though any of this was funny! He quickly slid past the crowd to get to the back and put in my order. He returned with a fresh crisp salad in his hand joined with a basket of hot steaming breadsticks. "Suga, I put in the order for your soup, it will be out in no time!"

A substantial amount of time passed. At this point, I could have found the original tomato garden and made the soup myself. "Just a few more minutes honey," he said and immediately turned to slide back to the kitchen. Finally, the soup arrived.

I rushed through grace to dig in. I expected this to be the best, most well-flavored and freshest soup I ever experienced. I leaned over the bowl as though I had absolutely no home training and attempted to savor my very first slurp, but the soup was not hot! It was not cold either, but, rather, it was lukewarm, the temperature of dishwater that cools down to a point where you question whether or not it is still sanitizing the dishes. My patience depleted from waiting on this soup. I kindly asked him for my check and a to-go bowl. Apologetically, my waiter provided me with the bowl and the check. As I rushed through the front door of the restaurant exit, bowl of lukewarm soup in hand. I felt a sense of great accomplishment!

I walked to my car, and I thought aloud, "I did it!" I partially fulfilled this strange desire for a meal alone and felt a pat on the back coming from Jesus for it. Perhaps he would compliment the patience I exercised or my generous tip; I deserved a little credit. I buckled in for the drive home, music low in anticipation of my pat on the back. "I have something more than partial obedience that I was looking for from you." He paints a picture for me recounting

the countless number of hurting people around me. I could see
that they could have used a smile or kind word, but I just passed by
in my "shameful singleness" hoping not to be spotted by someone.
Panning in on an elderly woman with snow white hair and mature
wrinkles that sat behind me in a booth, I remembered she was
all alone grieving. Disturbed by all that I missed, I quickly became
disgusted with myself. I was focused on what people would think
of me, but the real reason I was supposed to be there was so much
greater.

     I wanted to make sure I took God's order this time. In an
attempt not miss anything else, I pulled over in a grocery store
parking lot and grabbed my pen and journal out of my purse. I
began to take his order this time, just as the waiter took mine: "I
will take a hot drink because that which is warm, I will spit out of
my mouth. For my appetizer, I would like sacrifice, better yet, I will
have obedience instead. For my main course, I would like to have
thoughts such as these taken captive. Please let me know when
my meal arrives. I will not rush through grace because it is vital to
be pleasing. For dessert, I would like the chocolate layered love
cake." These words struck me deeply. I started my car back up to
drive home, rolled down the window and threw the soup as far as I
could, a bold outward declaration of throwing out that which was
lukewarm in my life.

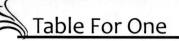

Prayer

*G*od, I ask for your forgiveness, and I thank you for who you are. Help me to be aware of the needs of those around me. You care about every detail, and I thank you I am not on a merit system for your love and affection. Take control of my thought life in such a way that my thoughts align with your thoughts. Allow me to think like you have shown me in your word in Phil 4:18. Help me focus my attention on the amazing and wonderful things of you. Show all the areas of lukewarmness so that my hands are clean and my heart is pure before you. Remind me of your grace as you forgive me for every time I have been so focused on myself that I did not recognize you. God, I thank you that your Spirit dwells on the inside of me, showing and empowering me to lay down and let go of those things which do not please you. Thank you for your sovereign grace. Amen.

Scripture

2 Corinthians 10:4-5
Romans 16:19
Revelations 3:16

Personal Reflection

Where are some places that you have allowed your thoughts to take you?

_____

_____

_____

_____

_____

What are you doing as you wait on your desires to be fulfilled?

_____

_____

_____

_____

_____

Are you living your life aware of the needs of those around you? What are they?

_____

_____

_____

_____

_____

What does the scripture in 1 Sam 15:22 mean to you?

_____

_____

_____

_____

_____

Thoughts

Encounter Nine:
The Repurchase

*T*he Lord speaks to me all the time. The challenge is not in His communication but in my listening. I get so busy sometimes that I rarely make the time to sit and just listen. But this day was a little different. In my listening and worship time, I began to daydream. A movie unfolded in my mind. I became a spectator in a story that He was unfolding in front of me. It was like the movie Ghost, but not in the odd, mystical way. In this dream, I was able to see myself, hear my thoughts and see my corresponding actions. The dream started as my car pulled into in a parking lot. I reached in the back seat to pull out a pair of shoes. I had a huge smile on my face; I could tell that these were a killer pair of shoes. They looked slightly worn, though. Maybe I walked in them out of the store and upstairs to my apartment. There was some light residue left by the price sticker. The shoes must have been on display. The lid on the shoe box was also loose and a little torn. I prepared myself to stroll into this massive shoe store. It was like a DSW on steroids! The store was called Gilda Grace Collections.

There were walls and walls of shoes, purses, and coordinating accessories. I was in awe! I was seriously thinking about moving in! I spent hours perusing the aisles and looking at all that the store had to offer, but it seemed like no time at all. There were pink shoes with red stripes on the heels, earrings that looked like they cost a fortune, and purses made by Prada, Gucci, and Louis. I even recognized unique items created by the owners of the store. With excitement, I explored every aisle, visiting some aisles even three or four times.

There were people all over the store, but I was completely unfazed by them. But I did see myself complementing countless women on their shoes, bags, and accessories. I located every mirror in the store to see how I looked when trying on all the items I wanted. I felt and looked great! Finally, after hours, I arrived in line, waiting for my turn at the counter. Surprisingly, with all that I had to choose from, I ended up at the front of the line with only one pair of shoes. These shoes looked familiar to me, even as an outsider. I must have tried on 1,000 pairs of shoes, and I ended with one pair.

I approached the register. While talking to the clerk about what a great store this was, my face showed pure elation. I dug deep inside my purse to locate my wallet. I was thinking about the many places I would go in these shoes, and I was mentally visualizing the many outfits I have that already match the shoes. Lost in my own thoughts, from the corner of my eye, I see the strangest look from the girl behind the counter.

"So sorry, it's such a big purse. I know my wallet is here," I said as if I were validating the fact that I was trying to hurry. Then, again, she looks at me in the strangest way. "Where did you find these shoes?" she says. "Oh, I brought them in with me," I say. Seeing the look of mass confusion on her face, she peers over her glasses at me as she says, "You brought these in with you and you would like to re-purchase them?" I say, "Yes!" I see the clerk is dumbfounded. She goes on to explain what happens when you make a purchase.

"Ma'am, if you have already purchased something, you do not have to purchase it again." I stood there dazed and confused as to what was going on. The scene ends. There was no closure; it's like the story abruptly ended. That was it. Really.

There has to be more. I mean why on earth would someone ever do that? God, how dumb is that? Who tries to purchase something that has already been paid for? There is no store that has a line for "Re-purchase." That would be silly! I went on and on in this rant about the silliness and how dumb it was. I just considered this entire daydream to be a dumb, distracting thought in the middle of worship. Then as I continued in worship, I felt like the Lord said, "My daughter, you live that way right now in relation to me."

Me? A sense of strong conviction came as I burst out in tears. I treat God that very same way. I would say things like, "God, will you please give me wisdom? How much work needs to be done for you to accept my sacrifice?" I cried out to God and said so many prayers for healing, strength, and deliverance, prayers for more godliness, insight, and understanding. I prayed for things like dominion and authority, power, revelation, and knowledge. I am not saying that we don't need to go before God. I felt in my heart that the message for me was clear. I don't have to re-purchase what belongs to me. The cross fully paid for the promises that are mine in God's word.

Think of the things you keep asking for, then ask the Lord to show you what already belongs to you. Pray that God would make you fully aware of the price he paid for your life. Ask for the Lord to reveal the power and authority that belongs to you and to give you the courage to fully operate in it.

My prayer for you is just that.

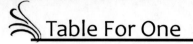

Prayer

*G*od, I thank you that I have been bought with a price that never loses value. I thank you that you take delight in me because you created me. My acceptance comes from you. I am secure in your love that requires me to simply trust. I thank you that you have already given me all the tools that I need for godliness and holiness to run the race that you have set before me. Continue to work in my life in tangible ways that I may realize how deep, wide and great your love is for me. At the cross you promised that you would send your Spirit to unveil the mysteries and the things of your heart. Lord unveil my value and provide me with the fortitude to walk in it. Amen

Scripture

Ephesians 3
Matthew 7:9-12
Psalms 139:14
Psalms 37:4

Personal Reflection

What does it look like when you find yourself trying to earn Gods love and acceptance?

_____

_____

_____

_____

_____

What price has God paid for your life?

_____

_____

_____

_____

_____

What promises from God do you cling to?

_____

_____

_____

_____

_____

What is your response when you pray about something but don't receive it?

_____

_____

_____

_____

_____

Thoughts

_____

_____

_____

_____

_____

_____

_____

_____

_____

_____

_____

_____

_____

_____

_____

_____

_____

_____

_____

_____

_____

_____

_____

_____

_____

Encounter Nine: The Repurchase

Encounter Ten: Misrepresentation

$\mathcal{I}$f I had to put a label on this season, I would deem it, misrepresentation. I could have blamed a few people for my arrival at this place and rightfully so because one person in particular, my pastor at the time, poorly presented Christ to me. This man used his authority to violate and scar me. I was hurting on the inside and I felt I had nowhere to turn, so I told a select group of people, some of which did not even believe me. This started the process of blaming myself and saying things like, "I made him look at me by serving on the praise team or wearing what I wore." Others knew that this kind of thing was going on, but tried covered it up at which point, my rose colored glasses were shattered and my perspective changed on everything, almost overnight.

I began living a misrepresented life; I did whatever I wanted, with whomever I wanted, whenever I wanted. My once soft, pliable heart was replaced with cold and numb replica of a heart after this violation. I felt so low and believed this was all that I was good for. I thought if that is all my pastor sees, then it must be true. I made a vow from that day on not to let anyone close, protect myself and push away anything that seemed too good to be true. I declared that I would never be deceived again! The vicious cycle of self fulfillment elevated to a whole new

level; this was a whole new ball game. I was going to hurt you before you could hurt me.

I had very little love, conviction or respect especially for
those in authority. If I did not agree with something that I was
asked to do, I would grumble, complain, verbally lash out or just
not do it, no matter what it was. This was a normal occurrence,
especially in the workplace when I took on my first job because
I felt like that was a joke too. A broken and directionless college
graduate that felt like she had nothing to offer, trying to figure out
why everyone wanted to use her or hurt her. I thought the salary,
influence and ability would make a difference. I ended up with this
crappy 8-5 and felt bamboozled!

I absolutely dreaded going into work every day, but the
thought of one relationship I built made it a little more tolerable.
Looking back on this experience, it was a truly a divine appoint-
ment to get me to this place. My coworkers and I clicked instantly
and became great friends. After a while, I went through the mo-
tions of being healed by being extremely clingy in a relationship
with someone who was never be able to please me, and I started
going back to church again, a church that was huge and no one
knew my name. I did not want to run the risk of something like that
happening again.

They had a big push for people to volunteer and before
seeking the help that I needed to overcome this issue or even let
people know that I was truly hurting, I signed up! I volunteered as
a leader with the youth, a true testament that God uses broken
people. All I had to do was show up an empty broken hot mess
and just hang out with the kids. They just wanted someone to care,
and I wanted the same thing. If I could keep what happened to me
from happening to them, I would make a difference. The services
were geared for the youth, but I felt like the message was for me
specifically, poor kids. Honestly, they turned out to be amazing and
I still have a relationship with the ones I was closest to, even today.

Things in my heart started to change a little. My coworker
knew that he saw something in me in spite of where I was at the
moment. I knew God's word because I had an amazing youth group
as a teenager, a mother who loves Jesus and a grand mother

who knew that she needed to lay me down at the cross. I would have long talks with my coworker, and he would often lovingly remind me that he was praying for me and ask questions like what do you teach your kids about living holy? Or can salt water and fresh water come out of the same fountain? Of course, I knew the answer in my head, but the problem was I needed something to change in my heart. His words were always seasoned with love, and I began to respect him more and more, as best I could.

Some time passed when I finally made the time to visit his church. The service was held in this old sanctuary that was converted from a gym and wreaked of smelly feet. Worship began with the lights dim and his wife leading. I closed my eyes and was swept away. I knew that this encounter with the Lord was long overdue. I literally felt like Jesus was right there with me. I broke down at the altar weeping for the first time in over a year.

I attempted to lay down the wall of hurt I carried to allow him into those inner places of my heart. My posture towards God was remorseful and somber as I prayed silently, begging for his forgiveness on one hand and demanding his vengeance for the violation on the other. "Why me?" I asked. I saw him pick me up, take me from my place at the altar and stand me up. He then put his hand gently on my cheek and began wiping my tears. He wiped my tears silently for as long as they would flow. I raised my head to look him in his eyes. I heard his strong authoritative voice say "I was there and I wept for you. I never wanted that for you and I am sorry!" I stared at him and responded, "Why didn't you stop it from happening and why did you let him hurt me?" With tears in his eyes, he said; "I am sorry, my daughter. That shame and misplaced guilt you have carried are why these scars are in my hands. That hurt you felt is why I had to come to be with my father so that you will have a place where you never have to experience that again. See, I know what it feels like to be hurt. I know what it feels like to be betrayed, mocked, laughed at and even spat upon. But, my daughter, I also know what it feels like to love and to forgive. The pain you felt was real and that pain is the fuel you will use to change nations. All those things that were bad; I am working out for your good. I know it is hard to see, but just trust me. I am going to my father for you."

This experience is what began my journey to healing and reconciliation. The hurt caused my perspective to change overnight; the journey I have been on has been one that has taken some work. So much so at times that I want to give up, but Jesus reminds me of this encounter giving me the strength and courage to continue on. I know that if he can do that for me, he can do the same for you!

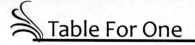

Prayer

ᒪord, help me not to tire on this journey and remember that you are not a God who is cold and distant. You are a God who is not unfamiliar with my suffering. Help me to not lose sight. Let those things that break you heart break mine. Thank you for mourning with me when I mourn and rejoicing with me when I rejoice. Help me to walk in love and forgiveness. God I confess to you right now that I have been unable to forgive _____ for _____and right now, I declare forgiveness over this person and/or situation. I trust that you know the end from the beginning and that you are the one who works all things for my good. Lord, in those times when I don't want to forgive others, remind me of the many times you have forgiven me. Amen.

Scripture

John 8:32,36
Luke 10:19
2 Thessalonians 2:15-17
Psalms 37:7-15
Psalms 119
2 Samuel 7:22
2 Samuel 22-51

Personal Reflection

Have you ever saw Jesus as someone who is familiar with your suffering? Explain.

_____
_____
_____
_____
_____

Has there been a time in your life when you went to God angry and questioned why? If yes, what was the outcome?

_____
_____
_____
_____
_____

What violations in your life did Christ go to the cross for?

_____
_____
_____
_____
_____

What have been waiting to do until you got everything together?

_____
_____
_____
_____

Thoughts

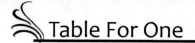
Notes From The Family

𝒥 always knew that Lahoma would definitely become someone very remarkable and successful. She has lived an extraordinary life and never had limits. I am very proud to know this book is written because her story is something that will inspire people to always set goals and let God have full control. God has blessed me tremendously with a sister who has conquered many challenges set before her. Every word written in this book will touch many lives as she has touched mine.

-Steve Dade

𝒥 think everyone that knows you can agree that words really don't justify your amazingness! I have never left your presence not feeling empowered to go conquer the world and knowing that I am an amazing woman and loved! I have never had anyone take personal time aside just for me, to challenge me to be the best Claudia that I can be. Your ability to pour into people's lives in such an impactful way is beside me, but I'm just thankful that I have been blessed as one of the recipients! I personally want to thank you for being an inspiration and role model to me. You have paved the way of excellence for our family by being the first college graduate and took the limits off of all possibilities, and because of that there is no room or excuses left for failure! I will never forget when you said, "Well who is "they?"" Since that day I made up in my mind that I would no longer let other people and life circumstances determine my success, life, and happiness. It has been one of the best decisions I have made in my life, and I have you to thank for that! I know this is only the beginning of your great accomplishments in life and will be the first of many seeds that will be planted into peoples lives. I could literally go on and on about how awesome you are and what you have been in my life, but then it would be a book inside a book so I'll stop here! I love you tremendously favorite cousin!

-Claudia Williamson

For those of you that may not know my little sister, Lahoma, I think you should know that she is a over achiever, strong as a bull and just as stubborn . She has a pure heart, speaks her mind and goes after what she wants. She can brighten a room with her smile. If you say it cannot be done, she will make it happen. She is one of my best friends and if you mess with her, you mess with me. I love my little sis and wish you the best.

-Corey Dade

I want to thank all the readers of my daughter's book. May God richly bless you. I wanted to give a little insight of who Lahoma is now and was as a child: giver, trainer and leader. Lahoma's brothers called her bossy,but very humble. This book was not an over night achievement; it was years of learning and prayer.

As her mother, I always wanted more for my children than what I had and for them to be all they could be! At 3-years-old, Lahoma was baptized and was dedicated at two-weeks-old to God. I was not qualified to make her what she needed to be, so I just trusted God all the way. I would tell her all things will work together for the good of those who love the Lord.

During my long illness, that I am still overcoming, I knew that my child(ren) would be fine. I still asked God for more time to see what he had decided for them. I thank God for my wonderful daughter. I cannot find the words to express my feelings for her. In closing, a quote from SATCHMO "Love like you have never been hurt ." When you don't understand your child, call on Jesus because I know that every thing will be alright. My desire is that I am hoping that God fulfills next is the husband he has specifically for her and a few grandchildren.

Signed the happiest and proudest mother in the world.

-Audrey Robinson

$\mathcal{I}$ have always been very proud of Lahoma. At such an early age I would always tell her how proud she made me feel. I know it was hard for her to believe me because I would tease her by saying she was found under a rock. WOW, what a hard word from a dad who calls his daughter "Sunshine."

She is truly a tomboy at heart who would put fear into her older brothers' hearts. The times we spent together were often at my mother's apartment. My mother spent many hours talking about her love for Jesus Christ as she would prepare for her Sunday school class. As the years went by we would have our couch-side chats. I could feel the presence of the spiritual growth within her. Found under a rock, now stands next to the "Rock" Jesus Christ.

-Homer Dade

$\mathcal{I}$ just wanted to let you know how much I love you and that I thank God every time I'm with you for putting you in my family. You have done so much for me these last few years, and I really appreciate it.

If it weren't for you, more than likely I would not be in college or have a steady job. You talked to me and helped me figure out what I wanted to do with my life. You are one beautiful and amazing woman and you deserve everything that comes your way.

Love you for ever and always.

-Shakena Powell

$\mathcal{T}$ here are not enough words to describe how great Lahoma truly is. Lahoma is the most selfless person I know. Her number one goal is to always make sure others fulfill their goals and destiny and somehow she still manages to fulfill hers as well after giving so much of herself. Lahoma takes "the excuse" out of every equation making every goal achievable and reasonable. She's the one you go to when you need direction, love, encouragement, support and an unbiased opinion. Out of all of great qualities Lahoma possess, the one that sticks out the most is the fact that she's able to embrace that she's able to embrace every situation, learn from it and teach others about it. I thank God on a regular basis to have such a wonder woman of God in my life. She has filled many absent roles in my life, the number one being a mother. She's always been sure to let me know my potential, ensure my success and has always allowed me to feel loved even when I didn't love myself. Although, I'm family... anyone who comes in contact with Lahoma is sure to receive the same love and it always comes with a smile and hug. I can't wait to see what else God has in store for her, I know her destiny is limitless.

-Andrea Williamson